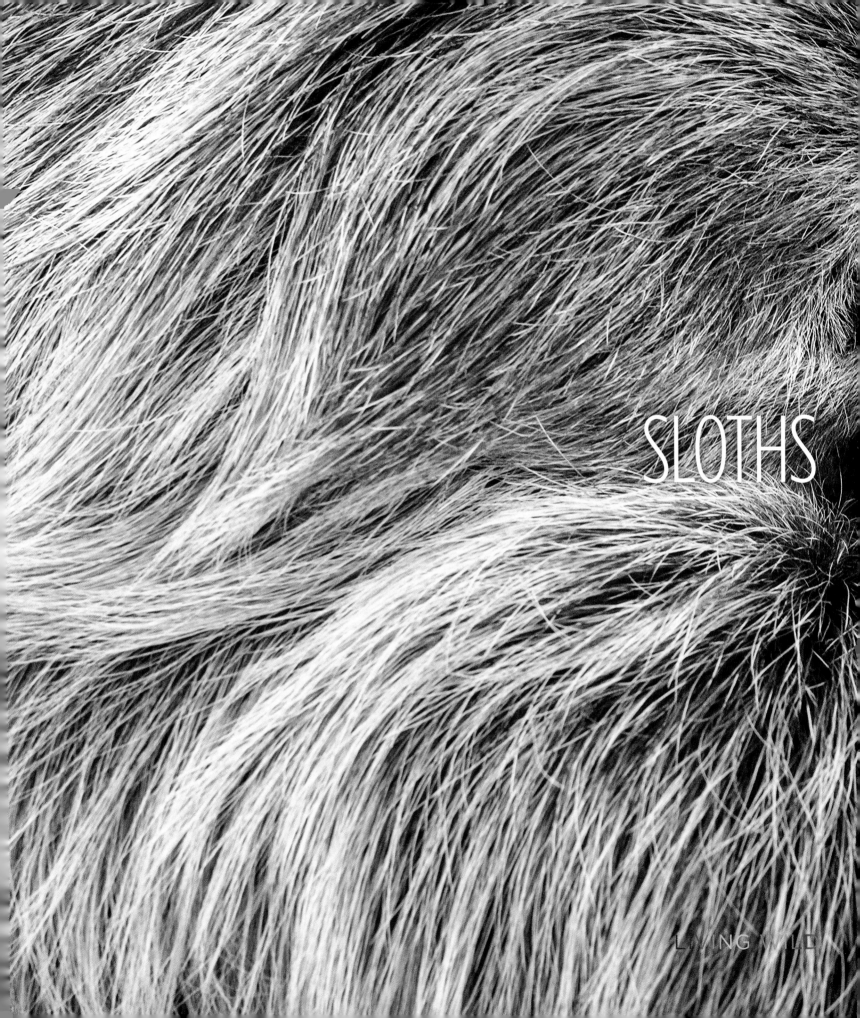

SLOTHS

LIVING WILD

Published by Creative Education and Creative Paperbacks
P.O. Box 227, Mankato, Minnesota 56002
Creative Education and Creative Paperbacks are imprints of The Creative Company
www.thecreativecompany.us

Design and production by Mary Herrmann
Art direction by Rita Marshall
Printed in the United States of America

Photographs by Corbis (Bill Hatcher/National Geographic Creative, Mark Moffett/Minden Pictures), Creative Commons Wikimedia (Adam.zolkover, Charlesjsharp, Paulo B. Chaves, Rusty Clark, Fernando Flores, Pearson Scott Foresman, G.dallorto, C. Horwitz and Steven G. Johnson, Dave Pape, Klaus Rassinger and Gerhard Cammerer), Dreamstime (Amilevin, Lukas Blazek, Isaacschaal, Vrabelpeter1), iStockphoto (Aunt_Spray, danefromspain, Patrick Gijsbers, Keith Hinman, IMPALASTOCK, Mark Kostich, MsLightBox, pchoui, Snic320), NASA (Rob Simmon), Shutterstock (7877074640, Edwin Butter, Rafal Cichawa, Cuson, Pavel Hlystov, Matthew W Keefe, Inga Locmele, Nagel Photography, S.A., Martijn Smeets, Paul Strehlenert, Elfred Tseng, Joost van Uffelen, UltraOrto, Vilainecrevette, worldswildlifewonders)

Library of Congress Cataloging-in-Publication Data
Gish, Melissa.
Sloths / Melissa Gish.
p. cm. — (Living wild)
Includes bibliographical references and index.
Summary: A look at sloths, including their habitats, physical characteristics such as their long claws, behaviors, relationships with humans, and their growing popularity in the world today.

ISBN 978-1-60818-709-6 (hardcover)
ISBN 978-1-62832-305-4 (pbk)
ISBN 978-1-56660-745-2 (eBook)
1. Sloths—Juvenile literature. I. Title. II. Series: Living wild.

QL737.E2 G57 2016
599.3/13—dc23   2015026882

CCSS: RI.5.1, 2, 3, 8; RST.6-8.1, 2, 5, 6, 8; RH.6-8.3, 4, 5, 6, 7, 8

HC 9 8 7 6 5 4 3 2
PBK 9 8 7 6 5 4 3 2 1

CREATIVE EDUCATION • CREATIVE PAPERBACKS

SLOTHS

Melissa Gish

A pygmy three-toed sloth clings to a high mangrove

branch on the Panamanian island of Escudo de Veraguas.

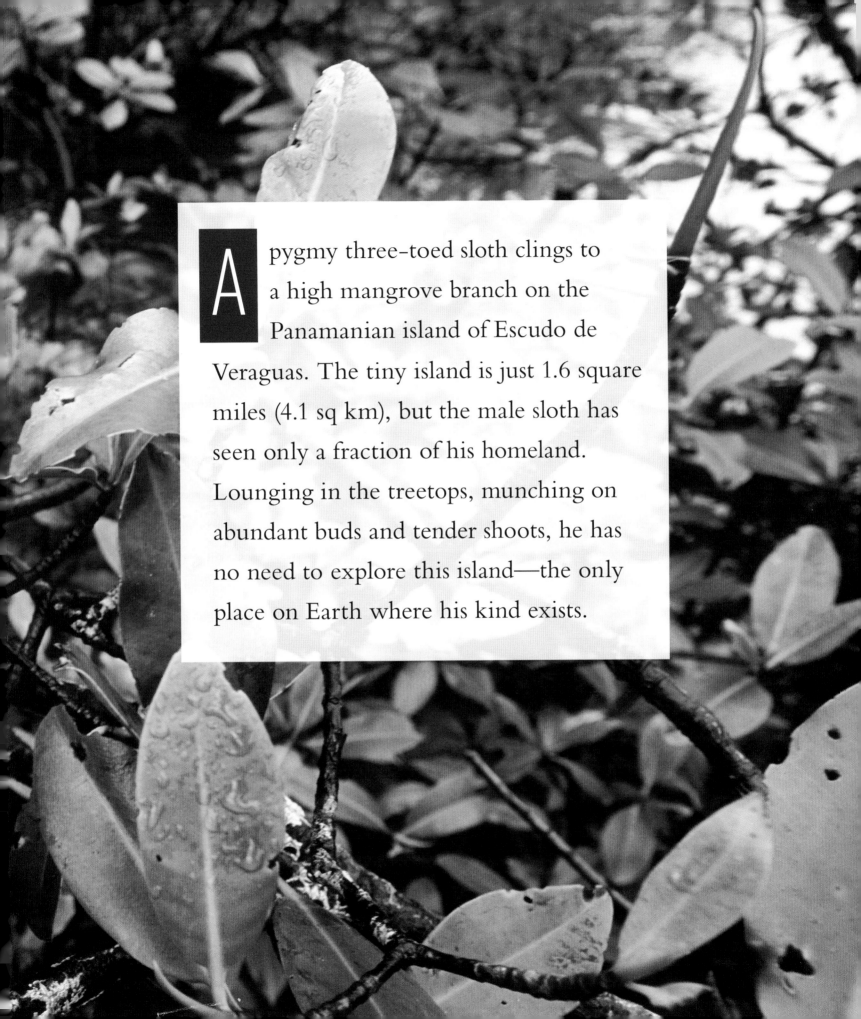

A pygmy three-toed sloth clings to a high mangrove branch on the Panamanian island of Escudo de Veraguas. The tiny island is just 1.6 square miles (4.1 sq km), but the male sloth has seen only a fraction of his homeland. Lounging in the treetops, munching on abundant buds and tender shoots, he has no need to explore this island—the only place on Earth where his kind exists.

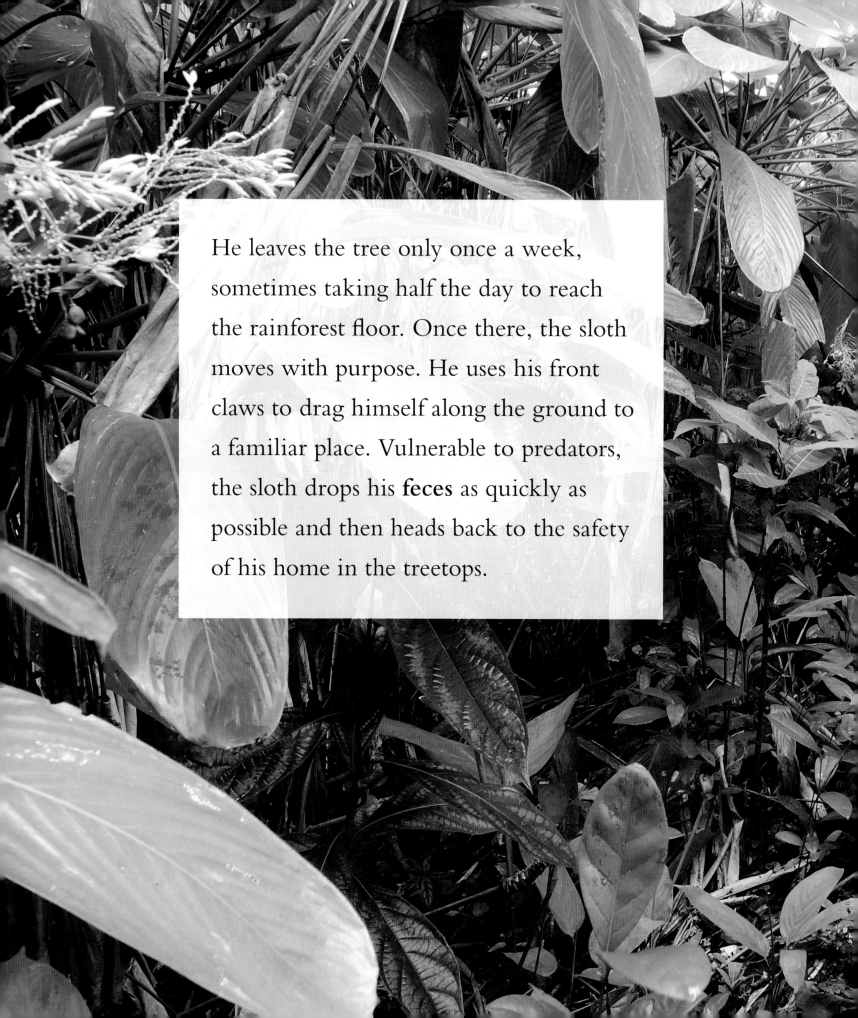

He leaves the tree only once a week, sometimes taking half the day to reach the rainforest floor. Once there, the sloth moves with purpose. He uses his front claws to drag himself along the ground to a familiar place. Vulnerable to predators, the sloth drops his **feces** as quickly as possible and then heads back to the safety of his home in the treetops.

WHERE IN THE WORLD THEY LIVE

■ **Hoffmann's Sloth**
southern Central America through northwestern South America

■ **Linnaeus's Sloth**
northern South America

■ **Brown-throated Sloth**
southern Mexico through southern Brazil

■ **Pale-throated Sloth**
Venezuela and northern Brazil

■ **Maned Sloth**
Atlantic coast of southeastern Brazil

Six sloth species inhabit the rainforests of southern Central America and northern South America. Two-toed and three-toed sloth populations vary from the vulnerable maned sloth, found only in southeastern Brazil's Atlantic coastal forests, to the stable population of the brown-throated sloth, which ranges from southern Mexico through southern Brazil. The colored squares represent the areas in which five kinds of sloths can be found in the wild today.

WEIRD AND WONDERFUL

The giant anteater (above) and three other anteater species are the sloth's closest relatives.

Hanging upside down from tall trees or moving in what appears to be slow motion, sloths are some of the weirdest creatures in the animal kingdom. They are found only in Central and South America, where they live high in the rainforest **canopy** as folivores (animals that mainly eat foliage, or leaves). Sloths were named by 16th-century Spanish explorers who visited the Americas. The Middle English word "slouthe" (*SLOOTH*) emerged in the 12th century, derived from an Old English word meaning "slowness." Seeing the strange, slow-moving creatures in the forest, the explorers called them "slouthes," which eventually became "sloths." The word "sloth" also means laziness, but sloths are not lazy—they simply **evolved** to have an ultra-slow lifestyle.

Sloths and their closest relatives, anteaters and armadillos, are **mammals** classified in the superorder Xenarthra (*zee-NARTH-ra*), meaning "strange joints." These mammals have extra joints in their backbones. Sloths also have extra neck vertebrae, which allows them to swivel their necks 270 degrees. This means they can keep their heads right-side up while their bodies are

Short back legs prevent the Hoffmann's and other sloths from moving quickly on the ground.

A sloth's body mass is only 25 percent muscle, which is less than half as much muscle as most other mammals.

hanging upside down. The six species of sloth are divided into two groups: Megalonychidae (two-toed sloths) and Bradypodidae (three-toed sloths).

The two-toed sloths include the Hoffmann's (named for German naturalist Karl Hoffmann) and Linnaeus's (named for Swedish scientist Carl Linnaeus) sloths. As their group's name implies, these sloths have two long claws on each front paw (and three on each back paw). Two populations of Hoffmann's sloth exist. One ranges from Honduras to Ecuador; the other lives in Peru, western Brazil, and Bolivia. The Linnaeus's sloth is found from Ecuador to the Atlantic coast.

Two-toed sloths have five to seven neck vertebrae. They have long, bare muzzles with piglike snouts and shaggy cream or golden-brown fur. Two-toed sloths typically grow 21 to 28 inches (53.3–71.1 cm) long and weigh 10 to 20 pounds (4.5–9.1 kg). Females are generally larger than males. The sloths' short tails—usually no more than an inch (2.5 cm) long—are nearly invisible beneath their long fur. Their claws are typically 2 to 2.5 inches (5.1–6.4 cm) in length.

Three-toed sloths are named for the three claws on

The Linnaeus's two-toed sloth is the largest and fastest moving of all sloth species.

Male maned sloths have a longer, darker mane of fur running down their backs than female maned sloths.

each paw. Their front limbs are about 35 percent longer than their back limbs. Brown-throated sloths have the largest range, from southern Mexico to southern Brazil. Pale-throated sloths inhabit Venezuela to northern Brazil, while maned sloths are found only in the Atlantic coastal forests of southeastern Brazil. Pygmy sloths were identified as a unique species in 2001. They are found solely on Panama's island of Escudo de Veraguas. Fewer than 100 pygmy sloths exist, making them some of the rarest animals on Earth.

Three-toed sloths have eight or nine neck vertebrae. They have fur-covered muzzles that are shorter than their two-toed cousins'. Their grayish-brown fur has markings on the face, neck, and back, depending on the species. Males develop a characteristic spot on the back when they are about a year old. A mane of black fur runs down the neck and shoulders of the maned sloth. Most three-toed sloths grow to about 18 inches (45.7 cm) in length and weigh 8 to 10 pounds (3.6–4.5 kg). Their tails measure two to three inches (5.1–7.6 cm), and their claws, three to four inches (7.6–10.2 cm). Pygmy sloths are about 40 percent smaller than the other three-toed sloths.

A baby three-toed sloth is carried by its mother for about one month, when it stops needing her milk.

Because sloths have slow-moving blood, it can take them as many as four hours to warm up when chilled.

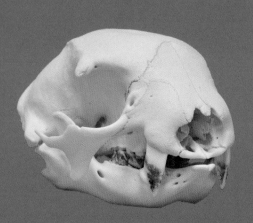

The sloth's sharp front teeth rip leaves apart, while its back teeth grind food to a pulp.

The Dallas World Aquarium is home to two brown-throated sloths, the only three-toed sloths on display in America.

This smaller size is the result of insular dwarfism, or a tendency for animals living on islands to become smaller in order to survive on limited resources.

The three-toed sloth's body supports a unique cycle of life. The sloth's fur has tiny ridges that hold moisture, creating an ideal environment for a special kind of algae to grow. Because the leaves and flowers that sloths eat are not very nutritious, sloths need to supplement their diet by eating the algae on their fur. Pyralid moths also live in sloths' fur. These moths provide nitrogen that keeps the algae growing. Three-toed sloths descend to the ground once a week to defecate, and during these times, the moths drop their eggs into the sloth's feces. The eggs hatch into **larvae** that feed on the feces. The larvae then develop into adult moths. During another of the sloth's descents, the moths fly into the sloth's fur, continuing the cycle of algae growth. Because two-toed sloths defecate from the treetops, they harbor fewer algae and moths.

Sloths have just 18 teeth (while most other mammals have at least 30). The two top front blade-like teeth are for biting. The upper and lower jaws each have eight peg-

like teeth for chewing. Because the teeth have no hard, protective coating, they wear down easily. However, since sloths typically eat only soft leaves, shoots, and flowers, they have little need for hard, grinding teeth. Sloths do not have baby teeth that fall out like most mammals'. Rather, sloths' teeth grow slowly throughout their lifetime and are

Sharp claws dig into trees as the sloth's own body acts as a counterweight, holding the animal in place.

Three-toed sloths eat only leaves and flowers, whereas two-toed sloths sometimes add fruit to their diet.

kept sharp by rubbing against each other.

Because sloths eat food that is not easily digestible, special bacteria in the sloth's four-chambered stomach help break it down. The sloth's belly looks swollen much of the time because of the gas produced by digestion, and up to a third of a sloth's weight can be attributed to the contents of its stomach. Some foods can take up to a month to digest.

All sloths' ears are small and hidden by fur. Sloths have poor hearing and vision, but they have a powerful sense of smell. This is how they locate and learn about one another. Sloths spend much of their time upside down, moving hand-over-hand along branches or just hanging out. Their fur is suited to this lifestyle, growing from belly to back (opposite of other mammals'). This way, when it rains, water easily runs off the body. Sloths do not have strong muscles in their limbs or bodies—they don't need them. Muscles in their paws do all the work, locking their claws into a hooklike grip. In fact, their grip is so powerful that sloths have been discovered with their claws still wrapped around branches after they have died.

Sloths learn to map the trees in which they live to avoid climbing on weak branches and risking a fall.

Rough, hairless footpads help
sloths grip, since moist fur on
their feet would be slippery.

LIFE IN SLOW MOTION

T he average life span of a sloth is 15 years. Sloths prefer to live alone in an established area called a home range. Depending on the availability of food and the number of sloths populating an area, three-toed sloths' home ranges can be as small as just a few trees or as big as 16 acres (6.5 ha). Two-toed sloths may forage over areas of 350 acres (142 ha). Sloths' home ranges often overlap, though individuals generally stay away from each other. They move from tree to tree by gripping crisscrossed branches or canopy creepers, which are woody vines that make up much of a rainforest's plant life. In the treetops, sloths choose each movement carefully. They climb one to three feet (0.3–0.9 m) per minute. When feeling threatened, however, they can move 15 feet (4.6 m) per minute. Depending on the situation—whether casually moving to a new tree or sprinting to escape a predator—sloths can crawl on the ground at two to five feet (0.6–1.5 m) per minute.

While captive sloths typically sleep up to 19 out of every 24 hours, sloths in the wild are more active, sleeping only about 9 hours at a time. Two-toed sloths

Three-toed sloths' front limbs are 45 percent longer than their back limbs, helping them swim with ease.

Sloths can remain anchored in a tree with just one set of claws dug into a branch.

When a sloth sits upright, gravity moves heavier pieces of food to the bottom of the stomach, speeding up digestion.

are nocturnal, which means they sleep during the day and are active at night. Three-toed sloths are diurnal, meaning they are most active in daytime. Though sloths browse for food almost continuously while awake, they do so very slowly. Because their food offers little nutritional value, they cannot afford to waste energy. They rest often, usually sitting upright in the crook of a tree to aid digestion.

To further conserve energy, sloths maintain a low body temperature—approximately 86 to 93 °F (30 to 33.9 °C). Because they process energy very slowly, sloths cannot shiver to warm up like most other mammals do. If the environment becomes too cold, a sloth's body systems will shut down, making it impossible to digest food. This is one reason scientists are concerned about the effects of global **climate change** on the rainforests. Long periods of unseasonably cold weather can lead to sloth starvation.

When sloths sleep, they curl up in a ball pressed into the fork of a tree. This helps them hide from predators. Harpy eagles are a sloth's greatest enemy. With wingspans of up to seven feet (2.1 m), these birds of prey can maneuver through the forest to snatch sloths out of trees. The largest

snake in the world, the green anaconda, also preys on sloths. Stretching more than 29 feet (8.8 m) long, this tree-dwelling snake can easily swallow sloths whole. Sloths are most vulnerable during their descent to the ground to defecate or as they move to different trees. Big cats such as jaguars, margays, and ocelots effortlessly kill sloths. A sloth's only defense is its sharp claws, but with weak muscles, these animals inflict little damage on enemies.

Research suggests that sloth feces contain chemical signals that tell a sloth's gender, age, and a female's

Research published in 2007 revealed that sloths in the wild sleep far less than previously thought.

Despite the threat of predators, male sloths move on the ground when seeking a screaming female.

readiness to mate. If a male smells the feces of a female at the base of a tree, he knows a female must be above. This is useful for mating, the only time when sloths give up their solitary lifestyle. Sloths have no seasonal mating period. Females can go into heat and become pregnant at any time of the year. Females reach sexual maturity around age three, but males are not ready to mate until they are four or five. When a female wants to mate, she lets out a piercing scream that can be heard by males nearly half a mile (0.8 km) away. The closest males will descend from their trees and head to the female's tree.

If more than one male seeks the female's attention, they may fight over the opportunity to mate. They will hang from a high branch by their back claws and bat each other with their front claws. The weaker sloth will either give up and move on or fall to the ground—sometimes resulting in death. Sloths practice a promiscuous mating system. This means that mating is a one-time event between a male and female, who each go on to mate with other partners. After a female becomes pregnant, she stops screaming, and males leave her alone once again.

Tightly interlacing branches allow sloths to move from one tree to another without having to climb down.

Sloth vision improves with age, but research suggests even adults cannot focus beyond five feet (1.5 m).

When sloth pups begin eating solid food, they learn which leaves are safe to eat by licking leaf bits off their mothers' lips.

The **gestation** period varies widely. Pale-throated sloths gestate for four and a half months and Hoffmann's sloths for five and a half months. Pygmy and maned sloths gestate for six months and brown-throated sloths for seven months. Linnaeus's sloths take the longest time to develop: 11 and a half months. The female gives birth while hanging upside down from a branch. Normally, one baby (called a pup) is born. Twin births are rarely seen. The Hoffmann's sloth is the largest newborn, weighing 12 to 14 ounces (340–397 g). Other sloth species are smaller.

Immediately after birth, the pup crawls up its mother's body to her chest, where it begins to feed on the **nutrient**-rich milk she produces. The pup is born with claws and uses all four sets to cling to its mother's body. When the pup is about 10 days old, it begins sampling leaves and flowers that its mother provides, though it continues to feed on her milk for another two to three weeks. When the pup no longer needs its mother's milk, it releases its grip on her body and moves about on its own. Sloths have a natural instinct to grip, but they must be taught how to move through the trees with coordinated, hand–over–hand movement.

Sloths are not picky eaters. To keep from ingesting the many poisonous plants and flowers in its environment, a sloth pup must learn from its mother which foods are safe to eat. It will stay with her for up to two years, growing stronger and learning to feed and defend itself from danger. As the sloth ages, it becomes braver and travels ever farther from its mother. When the time comes for it to leave its home for good, the young sloth will claim a portion of its mother's home range or move into an area vacated by another sloth.

Orphaned sloth pups in zoos and sanctuaries are fed goat's milk until they are old enough to eat solid foods.

Ridges on the tongue help the sloth continuously push food down the throat without having to stop chewing.

In the Amazon, sloths are called *ais* (EYES) for the sound of their loud screams. The name comes from the language of the Tupí, an **indigenous** people of Brazil who were driven to **extinction** by European settlers beginning in the 16th century. Although the Tupí **culture** disappeared, some of its language and folklore survived, handed down over generations to people of mixed European and Tupí descent. Today, the sloth is still known as "ai" in Brazil.

Another group of indigenous people, the Karajá, survives in present-day Brazil. A Karajá folk tale describes the sloth's carefree approach to life. Long ago, a terrible storm struck the forest. The ai fathers tried to protect their families from the storm, but the wind lashed at the ai mothers and babies, and the rain soaked them to the skin. As the mothers screamed in fear, the fathers all said, "We won't let this happen again. Tomorrow, we will build nests." The next day was sunny and warm. The ais soaked up the sunshine, slowly ate their breakfast, and napped for much of the day. They forgot all about building nests—at least until the next storm, when they

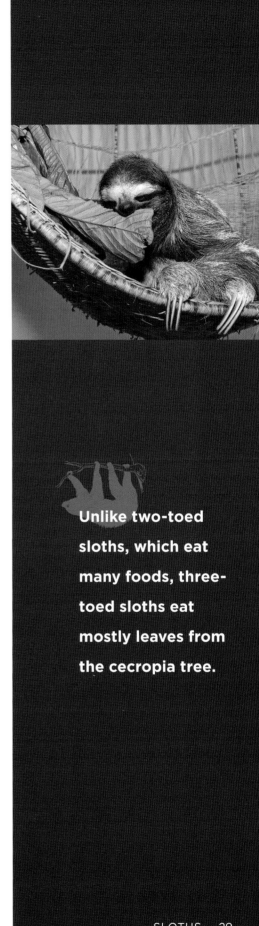

Unlike two-toed sloths, which eat many foods, three-toed sloths eat mostly leaves from the cecropia tree.

The sloth's claws close tightly on the paw, like pliers, which helps it maintain a grip on slender objects.

Most mammals store fat deposits around their bodies, but sloths keep extra fat only on the pads of their feet.

all said, "Tomorrow, we will build nests." Of course, the ais have yet to build any nests, for they spend so much time enjoying the sunny days that they forget about the few rainy days.

A **myth** from the Asháninka people of Peru and western Brazil explains the sloth's origins. Long ago, the earth and sky were closer together, connected by a long vine. A man named Pava lived on Earth but decided he wanted to live in the sky. He began climbing the vine. Some of his friends went with him. The rulers of the Earth did not want Pava to leave, so they sent their finest warriors—Kosámi, Tontóri, and Soróni—to pursue him. Pava and his friends reached the sky, where Pava became the sun and his friends became the stars. Then Pava cut the vine and sent the warriors falling back to Earth. Kosámi became the wasp and flew away. Tontóri landed on his arrows, which stuck in his back and turned him into the **prehensile**-tailed porcupine. Soróni tumbled into the trees, where he became entangled, his fingers and arms stretching like gum. He became the sloth, who moves through the trees with long arms and fingers.

Perhaps it is the sloths' unusual lifestyle or their cute faces, which look like they are always smiling, that have made them so well liked in popular culture. Sid the ground sloth first appeared in the 2002 Blue Sky Studios animated movie *Ice Age*. Then he was featured in four sequels to the hit movie, six video games, several short films, a television special, and even a live stage show. Sid is the smallest member of the *Ice Age* trio, which also includes Manny the mammoth and Diego the saber-toothed cat. He is clumsy, talkative, and not very smart, but he has a big heart. Despite being abandoned by his

Nicknames for sloths include cucala, unau, *and* prezoso de dos dedos, *which means "lazy with fingers."*

THE SHOES OF FORTUNE

. . . Behold—there are certain things in the world to which one ought never to give utterance except with the greatest caution; but doubly careful must one be when we have the Shoes of Fortune on our feet. Now just listen to what happened to the watchman.

As to ourselves, we all know the speed produced by the employment of steam; we have experienced it either on railroads, or in boats when crossing the sea; but such a flight is like the travelling of a sloth in comparison with the velocity with which light moves. It flies nineteen million times faster than the best race-horse; and yet electricity is quicker still. Death is an electric shock which our heart receives; the freed soul soars upwards on the wings of electricity. The sun's light wants eight minutes and some seconds to perform a journey of more than twenty million of our Danish miles; borne by electricity, the soul wants even some minutes less to accomplish the same flight. To it the space between the heavenly bodies is not greater than the distance between the homes of our friends in town is for us, even if they live a short way from each other; such an electric shock in the heart, however, costs us the use of the body here below; unless, like the watchman of East Street, we happen to have on the Shoes of Fortune.

excerpt from The Shoes of Fortune, *by Hans Christian Andersen (1805–75)*

family, Sid smiles optimistically in every situation—even if he doesn't fully understand it.

Another prehistoric ground sloth appears in the 3D animated film *The Croods*, released in 2013 by DreamWorks Animation. Set roughly 2.5 million years ago, the story follows a caveman family led by Grug as they deal with geological events taking place on the planet. They make new friends, including an inventor named Guy and his pet sloth Belt (so named because he spends much of his time wrapped around Guy's waist, holding up his pants). Unlike *Ice Age*'s Sid, Belt has very little to say. Mostly, he just smiles and comments with a little tune that simply goes, "Da da da!"

Real ground sloths inhabited the Americas until about 10,000 years ago. One mysterious creature is believed by some to be a remnant of those ancient beasts. Built like an enormous, shaggy, red ground sloth, the mapinguari is said to attack cattle and terrorize villagers in the rainforests of Brazil. Like North America's Bigfoot, the mapinguari's existence remains to be proven. American **ornithologist** Dr. David C. Oren, who works at the Museu Paraense Emílio Goeldi (a research institution and museum in Brazil),

Though they are protected by law in their native land, fewer than 20,000 sloth bears exist in the wild.

Sloth bears of India are not sloth relatives but are named for their calm temperament and long, curved claws.

Sloths are believed to be as intelligent as cats, able to recognize individual people and cry out to get keepers' attention.

believes the mapinguari—or something like it—is a real animal. He has trekked into the jungle numerous times over the past 20 years in search of it. British journalist Charlie Jacoby led a team of researchers to South America in search of the mapinguari for the 2006 History Channel *Digging for the Truth* episode titled "Giants of Patagonia." A 2011 episode of *Beast Hunter* that aired on the National Geographic Channel also featured a search for the legendary creature.

Real sloths are the stars of Animal Planet's eight-part series *Meet the Sloths*, which debuted in 2013. Each half-hour segment introduces a different element of sloth life at the Sloth Sanctuary of Costa Rica, the world's only facility dedicated to sloth rescue and rehabilitation. The videos can still be viewed online. Animal Planet's Sloth Cam, in partnership with Zoo Atlanta, features a live broadcast of the zoo's two-toed sloths—Cocoa and his two female partners, Bonnie and Okra, and their offspring. Cocoa has been recommended by the International Union for Conservation of Nature (IUCN)'s Sloth Species Survival Plan to breed with both females.

Sloths are admired and loved the world over. In Australia, wildlife expert Nick Baker hosts the show

Nick Baker's Weird Creatures, and in 2013, he included an episode titled "Pygmy Sloth." The animal proved so popular that Baker went to Escudo de Veraguas to make a full-length documentary, *The Pygmy Sloth of Panama* (2014). Though never broadcast in North America, the film can be viewed on YouTube.

Sloth pups at the Sloth Sanctuary of Costa Rica are returned to the wild as soon as they reach maturity.

Megalonyx *was a giant ground sloth that lived in North America from about 10.3 million to 11,000 years ago.*

FROM GIANTS TO PYGMIES

Nineteen different species of sloth once inhabited North and South America. Most became extinct between 5,000 and 10,000 years ago. Some were small, like modern sloths, but the largest were part of a group of ground sloths called *Megatherium*. They were some of the biggest mammals to ever inhabit Earth. The largest of these creatures was 20 feet (6.1 m) long from head to tail and weighed nearly 9,000 pounds (4,082 kg). Its claws were so long and curved that it had to walk on the sides of its paws. It used these claws to reach up into trees and pull down branches for food. Despite being nearly as slow-moving as modern sloths, *Megatherium* had no natural enemies. Even saber-toothed cats were no match for these enormous ground sloths.

In addition to helping scientists learn about sloth evolution, *Megatherium* has also provided a better understanding of human prehistory. It is widely believed the first humans traveled from Asia to North America by crossing the Bering **Land Bridge** 12,000 to 15,000 years ago. But in 2013, paleontologists at Uruguay's Universidad de la República made a sloth discovery that offered a new

Prehistoric humans traveled from Asia to North America by walking across the frozen waters of the Bering Strait.

Several species of marine sloths lived about 8 million years ago, feeding on aquatic plants just as manatees do today.

Sloths rehabilitated in a sanctuary often behave more socially than they would in the wild.

theory about how humans first populated the Americas. At a site in southern Uruguay called Arroyo del Vizcaíno, fossilized remains of giant sloths were found to have cuts and scrapes made by human tools. Further, piles of sloth bones were found together, suggesting the bones were purposely discarded in a trash heap. The bones are about 30,000 years old, which means humans would have arrived in South America much earlier than they reached North America, possibly by riding on rafts from Africa. One thing is certain: humans and giant sloths shared prehistoric habitats.

Most scientists agree that a number of factors, such as climate change resulting in habitat loss and overhunting by early humans, led to the extinction of ground sloths. Such factors continue to influence sloth populations today. While the hunting of sloths is illegal, poverty leads many people to hunt and trap wildlife to survive. The greater threat to sloths is habitat destruction. Enormous tracts of rainforest are destroyed daily for use in ranching, mining, and agriculture as well as urban development. While populations of two-toed sloths and pale-throated and brown-throated three-toed sloths are considered stable, other species are not so fortunate.

Maned sloths are being pushed into ever–smaller segments of habitat, where their **genetic** diversity is in jeopardy. In 2013, the IUCN classified the maned sloth as vulnerable, meaning that action needs to be taken to conserve the species. In graver danger is the pygmy three-toed sloth, classified by the IUCN as a critically endangered species. Although its island home is uninhabited, people go there regularly to harvest timber. In addition, the island is being considered for development as a tourist site, which would lead to roads, hotels, and other construction. With the population

The cutting down of trees for slash-and-burn agriculture does not give sloths enough time to find new habitat.

Gripping and climbing are instinctive to sloths, but learning which branches are safe is a practiced skill.

of pygmy sloths already perilously low, such human interference in the environment could swiftly wipe out the species.

One of the most serious threats to sloths today involves their cute demeanor. Worldwide demand for sloth pups fuels the illegal pet trade, particularly in Colombia, where the selling of exotic animals is the country's third-largest moneymaker after drugs and guns. Most sloths sold as exotic pets do not survive. Sloths require a specialized diet, and three-toed sloths in particular are susceptible to illness outside the rainforest. Even the most experienced **zoologists** have trouble keeping three-toes sloths alive in captivity, which is why so few zoos in the world keep these animals.

Living near people presents another challenge for wild sloths. As roadways cut through sloth habitats, many sloths get hit by cars as they relocate or try to reach water sources. When mother sloths are killed, orphaned pups have no way to survive except with the help of humans. Two people who have dedicated their lives to helping sloths are Luis Arroyo and Judy Avey-Arroyo. In 1992, they took in their first orphaned sloth, which they named Buttercup. As people brought more sloths to the Arroyos, the Sloth Sanctuary of Costa Rica was formed. The Arroyos and their staff have since rescued hundreds of sloths, some rehabilitated for release back into the wild and some that have become permanent residents.

The Arroyos knew nothing about sloths when they began, but now the sanctuary has grown into a research institution. In 2013, Rebecca Cliffe, a student from England, went to the sanctuary to begin a four-year research project for her PhD. Cliffe's research relied on a

Law enforcement officials cite the sloth's cute smile as a major reason people want them as pets.

To grip branches larger than three inches (7.6 cm) around, sloths must bend their wrists and ankles.

Sloths count on camouflage to help them blend into the background of their treetop habitats.

small electronic device called a Daily Diary, which was developed by British zoologist Rory Wilson. Called the Sloth Backpack Project, the research involved strapping the Daily Diary onto a sloth using a little backpack. The device could record data up to 32 times a second on each of its 13 channels. The backpack was later removed, and a computer program collected the device's information on the sloth's movement, behavior, diet, and energy use. Then the data could be used to help more sloths at the sanctuary return safely to the wild.

Another project launched by the Sloth Sanctuary of Costa Rica was an anti-sloth device for use by the country's power companies. Wild sloths often get electrocuted climbing on power lines. Using the sloths at the sanctuary to test various ideas, the Costa Rican Institute of Electricity found that big metal balls attached to the wires prevented the animals from being able to climb onto the wires. The sloths would bump into a ball and not be able to get over or around it, so they would have to back up and get off the power line.

Sloths are some of the most under-researched animals on the planet. In 2014, scientists at the Smithsonian

Tropical Research Institute in Panama found that fungi living in sloth fur combat cancer cells and the **parasites** that cause the deadly disease malaria. Undoubtedly, sloths have much more to share with us, but we must first help them survive in their fragile rainforest habitat.

Technology has recently allowed scientists to research sloths in the wild more precisely than in the past.

ANIMAL TALE: SLOTH GIVES FIRE TO THE PEOPLE

Today, most of Bolivia's roughly 5,000 Tacana people live in the rainforest and work as farmers and ranchers. Their ancestors, however, were foragers who survived on fruits, nuts, honey, and eggs. The following myth tells how the sloth taught the Tacana how to forage for food.

Long ago, the first people, called the Old Ones, had no knowledge of fire. They fed on wind and had no use for the forest's gifts. They smashed eggs and threw fruit in the river. When the animals saw the Old Ones coming, they hid from sight, for the Old Ones were cruel.

The children of the Old Ones were the worst. Once, they tied Python into painful knots and tossed him into a pit. Another time, they trapped Capybara in a dark cave.

Sloth watched the Old Ones' wickedness from the highest branches of the kapok tree. As the keeper of fire, Sloth's only tasks were to eat his fill of kapok leaves and keep fire safely away from the Old Ones. Everyone knew the Old Ones would misuse fire if they had it. Sloth left the tree only rarely to relieve himself. Sloth watched cautiously for the Old Ones when he descended to the ground. And he was very, very quiet.

One day, just as Sloth was about to climb back up the kapok tree, one of the Old Ones burst out of the underbrush. He captured Sloth and bound him to a long stick. Then the Old One dragged Sloth back to his village as a plaything for his children. The children put Sloth in a tree, but it was not a kapok tree. The leaves were bitter and made Sloth feel sick. The children teased Sloth, throwing rocks at him and poking him with a stick. They refused to let him climb down the tree to relieve himself.

Sloth was typically mild-mannered and quite tolerant, but after many days of this torment, Sloth could contain his frustration no longer. He threw himself out of the tree, landing hard on the ground. The children of the Old Ones were shocked and leaped on Sloth, holding him down so that he could not move. He cried out, begging for mercy, but the children of the Old Ones only laughed and pounded him with their fists.

He did not want to do it, but Sloth had no choice. He released the fire he was keeping. The Old Ones were terrified, for they had never known fire. Flames quickly swept through the village, killing all the Old Ones and scorching Sloth's back.

Sloth immediately felt remorse. He wished to rebuild what he had destroyed, so he gathered up the ashes of the Old Ones and created a new kind of human—one who could be trusted with fire. Molded in the spirit of Sloth, these new humans became the ancestors of the Tacana people.

To this day, Sloth bears the black mark on his back from the fire that killed the Old Ones. And the generations of new humans, much kinder beings, no longer feed on the wind. They forage for fruit and nuts like Sloth. They respect the animals of the forest, and they use fire wisely.

GLOSSARY

canopy – the topmost leafy branches of a forest

climate change – the gradual increase in Earth's temperature that causes changes in the planet's atmosphere, environments, and long-term weather conditions

culture – the behaviors and characteristics of a particular group in a society that are similar and accepted as normal by that group

evolved – gradually developed into a new form

extinction – the act or process of becoming extinct; coming to an end or dying out

feces – waste matter eliminated from the body

genetic – relating to genes, the basic physical units of heredity

gestation – the period of time it takes a baby to develop inside its mother's womb

indigenous – originating in a particular region or country

land bridge – a piece of land connecting two landmasses that allowed people and animals to pass from one place to another

larvae – the newly hatched, wingless, often wormlike form of many insects before they become adults

mammals – warm-blooded animals that have a backbone and hair or fur, give birth to live young, and produce milk to feed their young

myth – a popular, traditional belief or story that explains how something came to be or that is associated with a person or object

nutrient – a substance that gives an animal energy and helps it grow

ornithologist – a scientist who studies birds and their lives

parasites – animals or plants that live on or inside another living thing (called a host) while giving nothing back to the host; some parasites cause disease or even death

prehensile – capable of grasping

zoologists – people who study animals and their lives

SELECTED BIBLIOGRAPHY

Forsyth, Adrian. *Nature of the Rainforest: Costa Rica and Beyond*. Ithaca, N.Y.: Comstock Publishing Associates, 2008.

National Geographic. "Three-Toed Sloth." http://animals.nationalgeographic.com/animals/mammals/three-toed-sloth.

Slothville: Headquarters of the Sloth Appreciation Society. "What Is a Sloth?" http://www.slothville.com/what-is-a-sloth/#.VgB32SBVhBc.

Smithsonian National Zoological Park. "Meet Our Animals: Two-Toed Sloth." http://nationalzoo.si.edu/animals/smallmammals/fact-sloth.cfm.

Wainwright, Mark. *The Mammals of Costa Rica: A Natural History and Field Guide*. Ithaca, N.Y.: Comstock / Cornell University Press, 2007.

Vizcaino, Sergio F., and W. J. Loughry, eds. *The Biology of the Xenarthra*. Gainesville: University Press of Florida, 2008.

Note: Every effort has been made to ensure that any websites listed above were active at the time of publication. However, because of the nature of the Internet, it is impossible to guarantee that these sites will remain active indefinitely or that their contents will not be altered.

Like their animal neighbors, sloths depend on the health of their tropical rainforest habitats for survival.

INDEX